THE *Cheese* LOVER'S COOKBOOK

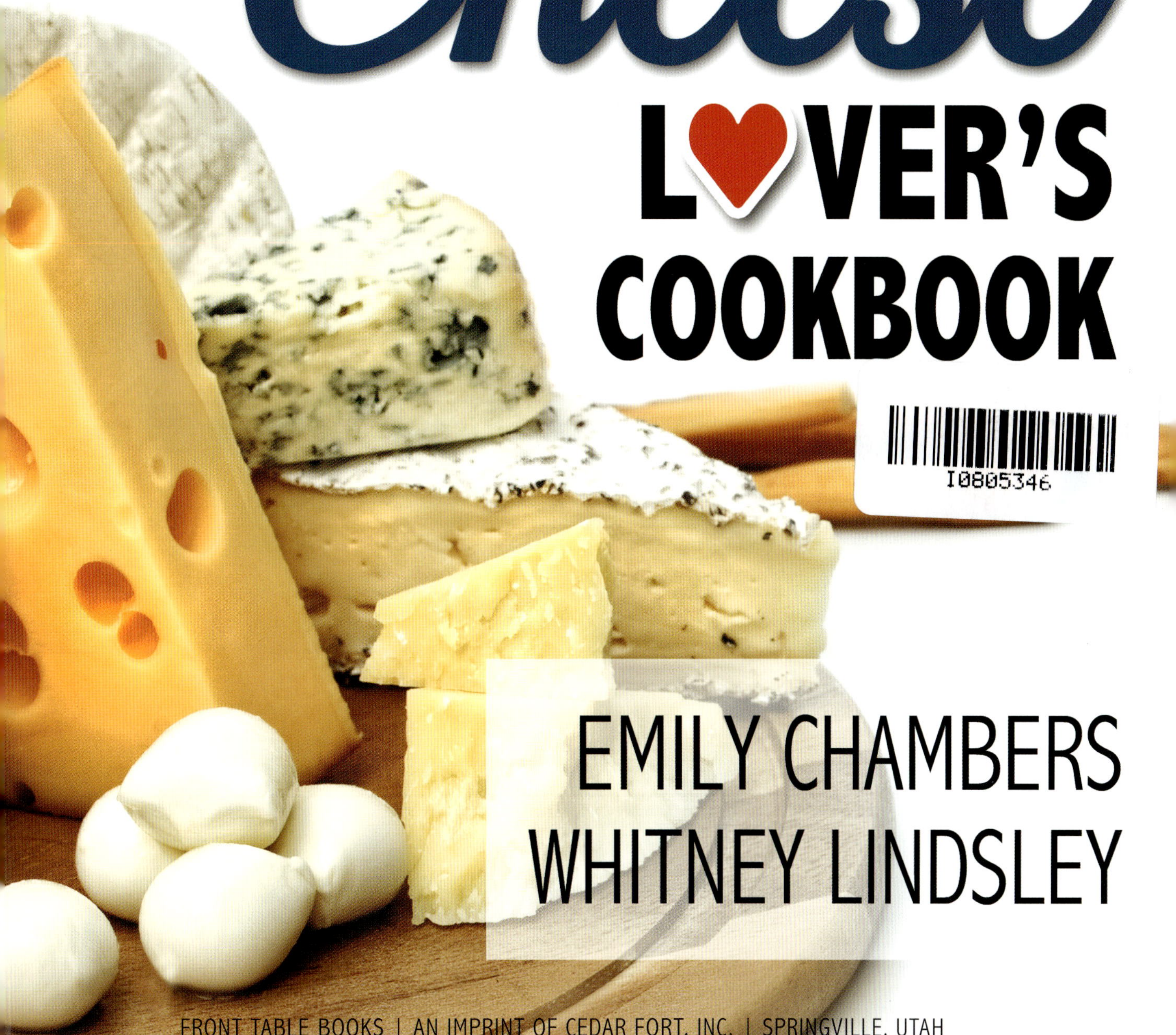

EMILY CHAMBERS
WHITNEY LINDSLEY

FRONT TABLE BOOKS | AN IMPRINT OF CEDAR FORT, INC. | SPRINGVILLE, UTAH

ISBN 13: 978-1-4621-1590-7

Published by Front Table Books, an imprint of Cedar Fort, Inc.
2373 W. 700 S., Springville, UT 84663
Distributed by Cedar Fort, Inc., www.cedarfort.com

Library of Congress Control Number: 2014959234

Cover design by Lauren Error
Interior design by M. Shaun McMurdie
Cover design © 2015 by Lyle Mortimer
Edited by Melissa J. Caldwell

Printed in the United States of America

10 9 8 7 6 5 4 3 2 1

Printed on acid-free paper

THE *Cheese* LOVER'S COOKBOOK

"Calling all cheese lovers! Chambers and Lindsley have created a fun book for when you are looking for some yummy, cheesy comfort food. *The Cheese Lover's Cookbook* has many great ideas for dinner, dessert, and for entertaining and would be a great gift for any cheese-loving friends or family."

—Victoria Skeem, Executive Chef for Culinary Crafts Catering

"What a wonderful resource for cheese lovers! The book is full of family-friendly and delicious foods. There's classic dishes, classics with a twist, and innovative recipes sure to please the cheese lover in us all."

—Christina Dymock, author of *The Bacon Lover's Cookbook, One Dirty Bowl: Fast Baking, Faster Cleanup,* and *The Hungry Family Slow Cooker Cookbook*

"This is one of the best recipe books I have seen in a long time. The authors have perfected recipes for a few classics and created many new recipes that feel like classics. I immediately wanted to make most of the recipes in the book! Far from being just another cheese cookbook, this book has a freshness and flair that make it well worth owning."

—Michele Nielson, cook and author of *Eat, Drink and Be Green* and *Dutch Oven Cookout: Step-by-Step*

"As a self-proclaimed cheese lover, I couldn't be more thrilled for *The Cheese Lover's Cookbook*! It's filled with creative and easy ideas for incorporating cheese into every meal. Emily and Whitney have hit this one out of the park. Yum!"

—Tonya Olsen, author of *Room Recipes*

"Chambers and Lindsley blend cheese expertise with culinary genius. These recipes are original, mouthwatering, and unapologetically cheesy. Soon to be your new favorite cookbook."

—Annie, Holly, and Chelsea Forsyth, *The Everything Naturally Sugar-Free Cookbook*, www.naturalsweetrecipes.com

To my mom, Susan; thanks for letting me be your little "Sue" chef. And to my husband, Joe; sorry for the indigestion. —Emily

To my parents, Bud and Mary Jo; thanks for teaching me how to cook and be creative in the kitchen. And to my husband, Rich; you're the best taste-tester. —Whitney

MYSHA DENS

Contents

Contents

Desserts

Acknowledgments

Emily would like to thank her husband for letting her do this crazy project. She also wants to thank her coauthor for being crazy and doing it with her. She'd like to express appreciation for her mom and her mother-in-law for teaching her about the true best ingredient to cook with: love. She also profoundly thanks Mysha Denson, her stellar photographer, for not only making her food look amazing, but also for being a taste-tester, friend, and just plain awesome person. (And thanks to Jason, Ella, Rivers, and Norah for sharing their wife/mom.)

Whitney would like to thank her husband, Rich, for all his support throughout the project. Without his great sense of humor and unwavering patience, this could've ended badly. She would also like to thank her coauthor for being awesome to work with on this enormous undertaking. Thanks also go to her parents for teaching her how to cook so many years ago. (Rich appreciates that too!) She would also like to thank the rest of her family for their love and support. Finally, a million and one thank-yous go to Nicole Fernley for her amazing photography and friendship.

They are both grateful to Cedar Fort for taking a chance on them as first-time authors, and to everyone there who designed and edited the book to make it really shine.

Introduction

RAISE YOUR HAND IF YOU LOVE CHEESE! Yes, that's what we thought, seeing as you are looking at this book. That's why we're bringing you many of our favorite cheesy recipes. There's just something about adding cheese that elevates the flavor of any recipe and gives it a certain flair. Think about using blue cheese on a burger. Or adding Parmesan cheese to make even a bland veggie inspired. Adds a gourmet touch, doesn't it?

Just to be clear, this isn't a book on how to make cheese. Many books out there outline this much better than we could and are written by professional cheesemakers. Instead, this is a compilation of gourmet comfort food recipes that each use cheese as a main component. We've tried to use all your favorite familiar cheeses, like cheddar and mozzarella, while throwing in a few specialty and foreign cheeses, like Gruyère and Emmentaler, so you can more deeply explore what cheese has to offer.

Cheese is a food that is used in so many different cultures that you'll find this cookbook has an international feel to it, especially paying homage to Italian, Greek, French, and Mexican cuisine. This variety helps even the pickiest palates find something they like.

If you're lactose intolerant, this is not the book for you. However, while this isn't a vegetarian cookbook, many of the recipes are naturally meat-free or can be easily adapted to be. Cheese is a great source of protein, and as we mentioned earlier, we've tried to make cheese the star or costar of each recipe to really let it shine. You can also use low-fat cheeses in many of the recipes to cut down on calories while keeping the integrity of each dish.

So from the Dubliner Puff Pastry Bite appetizers to the Berry Mascarpone Trifle for dessert, happy cooking and bon appétit!

— Emily and Whitney, the Gouda Girls

"AGE IS SOMETHING THAT DOESN'T MATTER, UNLESS YOU'RE A CHEESE." – Author unknown

Appetizers, Sides, and Salads

Cheesy Spinach Artichoke Dip

Serves 12 to 14

- 1 (8-oz.) pkg. frozen spinach
- 2 (6.5-oz.) jars artichoke hearts
- ½ cup mayonnaise
- 1 (8-oz.) pkg. cream cheese, softened
- 2 tsp. minced garlic
- ½ cup shredded mozzarella cheese
- ½ cup shredded Romano cheese
- ½ cup shredded Parmesan cheese
- salt and pepper to taste
- 1 cup shredded Italian blend cheese, reserved

This is great at parties! I never really liked artichokes before I had this dip, and now I love them. So if you're hesitant about spinach or artichokes, give this dip a try. You can also lighten things up by using Neufchâtel instead of regular cream cheese and light mayonnaise instead of the full-fat version. —Whitney

Preheat oven to 350°F. Prepare spinach according to package instructions (I prefer the microwave option). Let cool and transfer to medium bowl.

Use kitchen shears to cut up artichoke hearts in their jars. Add to bowl.

Add mayonnaise and cream cheese.

Add garlic, first three shredded cheeses, and salt and pepper. Stir mixture to combine, making sure all ingredients are incorporated. Transfer to a greased 1½-quart baking dish.

Sprinkle Italian blend cheese over top of dip and bake for 30–35 minutes, or until cheese on top is melted and dip is heated through. Serve with your favorite crackers or French bread cubes.

Romano cheese is an American-made cheese that derives from traditional Italian Pecorino Romano cheese. It is made from cow's, sheep's, or goat's milk, and is dry cured during production.

NICOLE FERNLEY

Chicken Cheese Puffs

The cheeses, onions, and garlic combine to make a delicious appetizer for any party. Better make up two batches—these go fast! —Whitney

Makes 12 puffs

- 1 can refrigerated crescent roll dough
- ½ (8-oz.) pkg. Neufchâtel cheese, softened
- 1 cup shredded cheddar cheese
- ¼ cup sour cream (scant)
- 1 tsp. minced garlic
- green onions
- 2 Tbsp. butter
- 1 cup shredded chicken (canned works fine)
- dash onion salt
- salt and pepper to taste
- 2 Tbsp. melted butter, reserved

Preheat oven to 350°F. Roll out crescent roll dough.

Mix remaining ingredients, reserving 2 tablespoons butter, in a large bowl.

Stuff each triangle of dough with chicken mixture. Place each chicken puff on a greased or lined cookie sheet.

Bake at 350°F for 12–14 minutes, or until golden brown. Brush with butter and serve warm.

New Zealand cheddar cheese is sharper and tangier than that produced in the United States.

Bacon Cheddar Cheese Ball

Makes 2 Cheese Balls

- 3 (8 oz.) pkgs. Neufchâtel or cream cheese
- 1 Tbsp. Worcestershire sauce
- ½ tsp. garlic salt
- ½ tsp. pepper
- 2½ cups sharp shredded cheddar cheese
- ½ lb. crispy cooked bacon, crumbled (8-10 slices)
- green onions, sliced
- slivered almonds

There was a time in my life when I didn't like cheese ball. Then I tried my mother-in-law's . . . Using real bacon and sharp cheddar is the secret. This is a variation of her recipe. Thanks, Vicki! —Emily

Cream the Neufchâtel in a stand mixer with the Worcestershire, garlic salt, and pepper until smooth.

Add the cheese, bacon, and onions, and mix until combined.

Divide cream cheese mixture into 2 parts and roll each part into a ball.

Roll in slivered almonds and then wrap each cheese ball in plastic wrap and store in refrigerator until ready to serve.

Serve with crackers or crisp veggies.

Similar in texture to cream cheese, Neufchâtel is a French cheese, and one of the oldest ones at that, dating back to the 6th century.

Fruit and Cheese Plate

A fruit and cheese plate or cheeseboard is traditionally served at parties and other get-togethers. The key to a good fruit and cheese plate is to provide variety and make sure any of your cheeses can be paired with any of your fruits, nuts, and crackers or breads. Offer a mix of soft, semisoft, and hard cheeses, and, as you get more familiar with cheeses, you can choose cheeses based on their flavor and on the other foods and beverages being served at your event. The cheeses listed can be found at the grocery store, but other hard-to-find cheeses (such as New Zealand cheddar cheese) can be found at specialty grocery and health food stores.

Choose two to three fruits (or two fruits and a spread), one cheese from each category, and two types of nuts, and serve with crackers and slices of baguette. Make sure to use a different utensil to serve each type of cheese, and slice pears and apples before serving (and sprinkle with lemon juice to prevent browning). Toothpicks can also be used for the semisoft and hard cheeses. In addition, cube hard cheeses and leave soft cheeses in their original form. Semisoft cheeses can be sliced or crumbled.

Fruit or Spread

apples, tart (Granny Smith, Braeburn, Gala, Jazz, Pink Lady)

cherries

dried apricots

figs

fruit jam

grapes (green and red)

grape tomatoes

pears (Anjou, Bosc, or Bartlett)

strawberries

Cheeses

Soft

brie

blue cheese

Boursin

Camembert

cream cheese

goat cheese (chèvre)

mozzarella

Muenster

Semisoft

Colby-Jack

Fontina

Havarti

Jarlsberg

Manchego

pepper jack

Semi-Hard/Hard

Asiago

cheddar

Colby

Emmentaler

Gouda

Gruyère

provolone

Parmesan

Baked Mozzarella Sticks

This is a great appetizer for kids and adults alike. The mozzarella gets warm and delicious while not completely melting and losing its shape. —Emily

Serves 4

12 mozzarella string cheese sticks
1 cup Italian bread crumbs
½ tsp. pepper
1 tsp. garlic salt
2 eggs
1 Tbsp. water
3 Tbsp. flour
marinara sauce for dipping

Preheat oven to 400°F.

Cut cold string cheese sticks to desired length.

In a shallow bowl, combine bread crumbs, pepper, and garlic salt.

In a separate shallow bowl, whisk together the eggs and water. Put flour in a third shallow bowl.

Coat string cheese in flour, dip in egg wash, and then coat in bread crumb mixture, followed by re-dipping in egg wash and bread crumb mixture.

Place on an ungreased baking sheet and bake for 7 minutes until golden brown.

Serve with marinara sauce for dipping.

Mozzarella is a semisoft cheese originally from Italy and is traditionally made from buffalo milk.

Cheese Fondue

The star of the party! Just add your favorite spices and serve with breads and vegetables for a fantastic appetizer to please any picky palate. —Whitney

Serves 6

- 1 Tbsp. minced garlic
- 4 Tbsp. white grape juice
- 1 cup milk
- 1 cup shredded Emmentaler or Jarlsberg cheese
- 1 cup shredded Gruyère
- 1 Tbsp. cornstarch
- 2 Tbsp. water
- spices to taste (basil, salt, pepper)
- assorted vegetables and cubed breads

Sauté garlic in grape juice in a medium saucepan over medium-low heat until fragrant.

Add milk, and heat until simmering. (If you need to increase the heat a bit, that's okay.)

Add cheeses slowly, making sure they are fully melted after each addition. Stir in a figure-eight pattern to avoid cheese sticking to the pan.

Dissolve cornstarch in water to avoid clumps. Add to mixture and continue to stir until thickened to desired consistency. Add more milk if needed.

If desired, stir in spices at this point. Transfer fondue into heated fondue pot.

If you don't have a fondue pot, transfer saucepan onto a trivet. Serve with artisan breads, vegetables, and cooked meats (e.g., steak or chicken).

If you need to reheat the fondue, please do so on the stove.

Emmentaler cheese is from Emmental, Switzerland. It is paired with Gruyère in traditional fondue recipes.

Ham and Swiss Cheese Ball

My dad always makes different cheese balls during the holiday season, and I created this one based on one of his recipes. Paired with your favorite crackers or veggies, this is a perfect appetizer for any occasion: Christmas, New Year's, Wednesdays . . . — Whitney

Makes 2 Cheese Balls

2 (8-oz.) pkgs. cream cheese, softened
1 pkg. ranch dressing mix
1 cup sliced ham, chopped
2 cups shredded Swiss cheese
2 cups chopped pecans

Combine cream cheese with ranch dressing mix in a medium bowl or stand mixer.

Add ham and shredded cheese and combine.

Divide mixture and shape into two balls, and then roll in pecans.

Wrap each cheese ball in plastic wrap and store in refrigerator until ready to serve.

Serve with crackers or crisp veggies.

American cream cheese was widely produced in the 1900s.

Saganaki (Greek Flaming Cheese)

Serves 6

- ⅓ cup olive oil
- 1 lb. Kasseri cheese (or provolone)
- 1 cup flour
- 1 lemon, cut in wedges

I hesitated to put this recipe in here because Kasseri, the cheese that is traditionally used, is a bit difficult to find. But ultimately, it's one of the recipes that inspired this cookbook, so here it is. You can order Kasseri online, but provolone works too. —Emily

In a cast-iron skillet on the stove, preheat the olive oil over medium-high heat until the oil is sizzling but not smoking.

Slice the cheese into ½-inch rectangles and run under cold water.

Dredge in flour and then place in the hot oil. Flip over after about 2 minutes and then cook on the other side. Cheese should turn golden brown.

Squeeze a wedge's worth of lemon juice on each cheese rectangle and serve immediately with pita or crusty bread.

Kasseri is most famous for being used in this traditional Greek appetizer, which is named after the cast-iron pan it is prepared in, a saganaki. Often when you order this at a Greek restaurant, it is brought out and served on the saganaki pan, flames and all.

Dubliner Puff Pastry Bites

This great little appetizer is paired wonderfully with sliced pears. —Emily

Makes 24 pastry bites

1 (9.5-oz.) box puff pastry cups, unbaked

¾ cup finely shredded Dubliner cheese

2 eggs

¼ cup milk

¼ tsp. salt

fresh parsley sprigs

Preheat oven to 375°F. On a parchment-covered baking sheet, evenly space puff pastry cups.

Bake for 20 minutes, until the cups have puffed up and started to turn golden. Remove from oven and use a wooden spoon handle to push in the centers of the pastry cups.

Distribute the Dubliner cheese evenly between all the pastry cups, filling them to the top.

In a small mixing bowl, whisk the eggs, milk, and salt together until foamy.

Carefully pour the egg mixture into the pastry cups, filling in around the cheese.

Reduce oven heat to 350°F and bake for 25 minutes; the middles should be firm and the crust golden brown.

Top with sprigs of fresh parsley.

Dubliner is an Irish cheese named after the city Dublin. It is a hard yellow cheese that is somewhere between swiss and Parmesan in flavor.

Cheeses

fresh mozzarella balls or cubes

Gorgonzola crumbles

cubed feta (the kind that comes in a block)

Parmesan or Asiago chunks or wedges

smoked provolone slices

Gouda wedges

Gruyère cubes or slices

Veggies

Kalamata or black olives

pimiento or garlic-stuffed green olives

tomatoes (grape or cherry)

pepperoncinis

marinated artichoke hearts

grilled zucchini or eggplant

fresh green or red pepper slices

pickles or cucumber slices

marinated or stuffed mushrooms

capers

arugula leaves

basil leaves

Meat

prosciutto

salami

any other thinly sliced cured meat

sardines, clams, or oysters

Breads and Crackers

focaccia bread

baguette or crusty bread

Italian hard breadsticks (grissini)

any variety of crackers or flat breads

Antipasto Platter

Antipasto in Italian literally means "before the meal" and marks the beginning of a traditional Italian meal. It's great to serve at parties before dinner's ready, or to be grazed on as an appetizer and throughout the meal. There are really no rules about what to put on an antipasto platter, but here's a slew of ideas that you can cater to your tastes and those of your guests.

The best platters have a good variety of cheeses, cured meats, vegetables, and bread or crackers. You can follow the same advice as for the Fruit and Cheese Plate and include soft, semisoft, and hard cheeses. And you can definitely be more daring and exotic with your cheese choices, but listed are cheeses that can be found at most grocery stores.

It's also nice to balance fresh vegetables with marinated or grilled/roasted ones, or even make spreads (such as artichoke dip or olive tapenade). And make sure to have some olive oil and balsamic vinegar close by, as well as cracked ground pepper and sea salt.

Queso Blanco

A rival to any restaurant queso dip. Serve with warm tortilla chips for an addicting appetizer. If you can't find white American cheese, look for the slices of processed "Swiss" cheese. —Whitney

Serves 8

- 1½ Tbsp. butter
- ¼ cup milk
- 12 oz. white American cheese
- ½ (4-oz.) can jalapeños
- 1 (4-oz.) can green chiles
- pinch garlic powder
- pinch chili powder
- pinch cumin
- salt and pepper to taste

Heat butter, milk, and cheese in a medium saucepan over medium-low heat, stirring occasionally, until butter and cheese are melted.

Add jalapeños, chiles, and spices, and stir to combine.

Serve warm with tortilla chips.

American cheese is technically not a cheese but a processed cheese food and gets its color from the spice annatto, which is added during the cheesemaking process.

Romano-Crusted Eggplant

Serves 6

- 1 eggplant (or 2 zucchinis)
- ½ cup bread crumbs
- ½ cup grated Romano cheese
- ½ tsp. garlic powder
- ½ tsp. paprika
- ½ tsp. salt
- ¼ tsp. pepper
- ½ tsp. oregano
- ½ tsp. thyme
- ½ tsp. parsley
- ½ tsp. basil
- ½ cup olive oil

My mom made me an early fan of eggplant with this recipe! —Emily

Preheat oven to 375°F.

Slice eggplant or zucchini into ¼-inch medallions.

In a shallow bowl, mix together all other ingredients except olive oil.

Pour olive oil in a separate shallow bowl. Dredge each medallion in olive oil and then cheese-herb mixture to coat evenly.

Place on a greased baking sheet and bake for 15–20 minutes.

Romano cheese is aged at least five months and is similar in taste and texture to Parmesan cheese.

Cheesy au Gratin Potatoes

These potatoes are a great side dish to any entrée. Add chives to really bring out the cheese flavor. —Whitney

Serves 8 to 12

- peeled Russet potatoes (about 6) or unpeeled red potatoes (about 8), thinly sliced
- 2 Tbsp. butter, cubed and divided
- 1 pint half-and-half, divided
- 2 tsp. garlic powder
- salt and pepper to taste
- 2½ cups shredded cheddar cheese (or cheese of your choice), divided
- 1 Tbsp. chives, optional

Preheat oven to 325°F. Grease a 9x13 baking dish with nonstick cooking spray. Layer half of the potato slices in the bottom of baking dish. Reserve ½ cup cheese.

Dot potatoes with 1 tablespoon butter. Pour half of the half-and-half over the top of potatoes. Sprinkle with garlic powder and one cup of cheese. Season with salt and pepper. Repeat process with remaining ingredients, except for the reserved ½ cup of cheese.

Bake covered for 30 minutes. Sprinkle remaining ½ cup of cheese on top and bake for an additional 30 minutes or until potatoes are tender. Garnish with chives if desired.

Wisconsin is known for its cheese production and produces the most cheddar cheese in the United States.

Cheese Pinwheel Rolls

Makes 16

Bread

- 1 cup warm water
- 1½ tsp. active dry yeast
- 3 Tbsp. sugar
- 3 cups flour
- 1 tsp. salt
- 1½ Tbsp. oil

Filling

- 2 Tbsp. rosemary
- 1 cup shredded cheddar cheese (or your favorite variety)
- 1 cup shredded mozzarella cheese
- 4 Tbsp. butter, melted, divided
- sea salt

It's hard to eat just one of these. So don't; eat two . . . or three.
—Whitney

Mix yeast with warm water until yeast is dissolved and bubbly.

Add sugar, oil, and salt, and stir to combine.

Add flour one up at a time until well combined. Cover and let rise for 45 minutes until dough is doubled.

Roll out dough into a rectangular shape on a floured surface.

Spread 3 tablespoons butter over dough. Add rosemary and cheeses.

Roll up lengthwise (like cinnamon rolls). Cut with serrated knife or unflavored dental floss (floss works better).

Line a baking sheet with parchment paper. Place rolls on cookie sheet.

Brush with remaining tablespoon butter. Sprinkle sea salt over top of rolls. Let rest for 30 minutes to let rise.

Bake at 350°F for 15–20 minutes until golden brown.

NOTE: You can also use your favorite pizza dough recipe for these rolls.

Mozzarella is available in a variety of forms, made from either cow's milk or buffalo milk, which is traditional.

Greek Feta Salad with Creamy Dressing

The first few times I had feta cheese, I disliked it for the strong vinegar taste. Then I found that if you buy it in block form, as opposed to pre-crumbled, it tastes much less briney. —Emily

Combine all salad ingredients in a bowl and set aside.

In a mason jar, combine all Creamy Dressing ingredients and shake vigorously until well blended.

Toss the salad in the dressing and refrigerate any leftover dressing.

Feta is a goat's milk cheese originating from Greece. It has a characteristic vinegar-type flavor due to the brine it is packaged in to keep it fresh.

Serves 6

Salad

1 head iceberg lettuce, chopped

2 medium tomatoes, chopped

1 small cucumber, sliced

⅓ medium red onion, sliced into rings

kalamata olives

pepperoncinis

8 oz. feta cheese (in a block, not pre-crumbled), cubed

Creamy Dressing

½ cup sour cream

¼ cup mayonnaise

¼ cup red wine vinegar

⅓ cup olive oil

1 tsp. sugar

1 tsp. onion powder

1 tsp. garlic powder

1 tsp. basil

1 tsp. oregano

¼ tsp. ground pepper

½ tsp. salt

Iceberg Wedge Salad with Blue Cheese Dressing

Makes 4

Salad

1 head Iceberg lettuce, rinsed and quartered (wedges)

1 cup diced tomatoes or sliced grape tomatoes

⅓ cup blue cheese crumbles

½ cup bacon bits

½ cup sliced red onions

Dressing

⅓ cup blue cheese crumbles

3 Tbsp. mayonnaise

1 (5.3-oz.) container plain Greek yogurt

¼ cup milk

salt and pepper to taste

A salad to make anyone feel fancy. The red onions add just enough of a bite to keep things interesting. —Whitney

Make salad by placing lettuce wedges on individual plates. Reserve tomatoes, bacon, red onions, and blue cheese. Set aside.

Make Blue Cheese dressing by whisking together all ingredients in a small bowl until smooth. (You can also use the mason jar technique found in the Greek Feta Salad recipe.)

Drizzle dressing over lettuce wedges. Top with tomatoes, bacon bits, onions, and blue cheese. Refrigerate leftover dressing.

Blue cheese needs to be stored in a regulated environment. Many blue cheeses are aged in caves, which are temperature-controlled environments.

Mozzarella Caprese Salad with Balsamic Vinaigrette

Fresh mozzarella with tomatoes and basil has to be one of the most inspired combinations of ingredients! For this recipe, make sure you're using the fresh mozzarella that comes in a big ball with a bit of liquid in the package—not the low-moisture kind. This is a great salad to serve guests on a summer day. —Emily

Serves 6

Salad

10 Roma tomatoes, cubed

2 medium cucumbers, cubed

16 oz. fresh mozzarella cheese, cubed

¼ cup fresh basil leaves

Balsamic Vinaigrette

¼ cup olive oil

½ cup balsamic vinegar

½ tsp. sea salt

¼ tsp. ground pepper

½ tsp. garlic powder

½ tsp. onion powder

2 tsp. oregano

2 tsp. thyme

Chiffonade the basil by using shears to cut leaves into ribbons.

Combine the tomatoes, cucumber, mozzarella, and basil in a large bowl.

In a separate small bowl, mix the olive oil, balsamic vinegar, salt, pepper, garlic and onion powder, oregano, and thyme to make the vinaigrette.

Toss the salad in the dressing, and serve.

Mozzarella cheese is the most popular cheese in the United States. American-made mozzarella is usually made with cow's milk.

"Antipasto" Pasta Salad

Serves 8

Salad

1 lb. uncooked pasta

1 medium green pepper, diced

⅓ medium red onion, diced

4 oz. black olives, halved

4 oz. green olives, halved

¼ lb. hard salami slices, quartered

12 oz. low-moisture mozzarella cheese, cubed

2 Tbsp. fresh basil, diced

1 cup grape tomatoes, halved

Dressing

½ cup olive oil

¼ cup balsamic vinegar

⅛ cup water

½ tsp. ground pepper

1 tsp. salt

1 tsp. garlic powder

1 tsp. onion powder

1 tsp. parsley

1 tsp. oregano

⅛ cup grated Parmesan cheese

I often don't love pasta salads. They usually seem bland or boring. So I set out to make a pasta salad that felt more like a meal and had lots of fun flavors and ingredients. I got my inspiration from a traditional Italian antipasto plate, which usually consists of cured meats like salami or prosciutto, olives, and a variety of sliced cheeses. —Emily

In a pot of salted, boiling water, cook the pasta until al dente.

Drain and rinse the pasta in cold water and put in a large serving bowl.

Add all the other salad ingredients. In a bottle with a lid, add all dressing ingredients and shake vigorously. Then toss the salad with the dressing.

Chill at least 4 hours before serving so the pasta can absorb all the flavors.

Part-skim, low-moisture mozzarella cheese is actually one of the healthiest kinds of cheese. It is low in sodium and saturated fat.

Goat Cheese Spinach Salad

Caramelizing nuts isn't very time-consuming and really makes a salad feel fancy. My sister and I experimenting with different fruits and veggies led to this refreshing salad. —Emily

Serves 6

Salad

12 oz. spinach

6 oz. goat cheese, crumbled

½ lb. strawberries, sliced

1 crisp pear, sliced

8 oz. mushrooms, sliced

¼ cup sliced red onions

Candied Nuts

½ cup sugar

1 tsp. cinnamon

¼ cup water

1 cup whole almonds or pecans

Combine all salad ingredients in a bowl.

To make candied nuts, dissolve sugar and cinnamon in water in a saucepan over medium-high heat.

Add nuts and stir constantly until most of the liquid has evaporated.

Pour coated nuts on parchment paper and allow to cool. Add to salad.

Dress the salad with a poppy seed dressing or Creamy Dressing (page 29).

Although we use cow's milk as the main source for making cheeses in the United States, goat's milk is the more widely used cheese source in most of the rest of the world.

"THE EARLY BIRD MAY GET THE WORM,
BUT IT'S THE SECOND MOUSE THAT
GETS THE CHEESE."

–Jeremy Paxman

Main Dishes

Ham and Cheese Breakfast Strata

Bake this strata first thing in the morning and you're sure to have a happy family. This is especially great on special occasions and reheats well in the microwave. Thanks, Angela Baxter, for this recipe! —Whitney

Serves 12

- 12 slices white bread
- ½ cup butter, softened
- 1 cup cubed ham
- 2 cups grated cheese (I like to use Colby-Jack)
- 4 eggs
- 3 cups half-and-half
- ½ tsp. Worcestershire sauce
- ½ tsp. dry mustard
- ½ tsp. salt

Butter six slices of bread and place butter-side down in a greased 9x13-inch baking pan.

Sprinkle ham and cheese evenly on top.

Butter remaining six slices of bread and place them on top, butter-side up.

Beat together eggs, half-and-half, and seasonings.

Pour mixture over the top of the bread and then refrigerate for several hours (overnight is best).

Bake at 325°F for one hour until eggs are cooked and cheese is melted.

Colby-Jack cheese is often half-moon shaped and can be used in a variety of dishes.

Serves 8

Dough

1¼ cup hot water

1 tsp. sugar

2 tsp. salt

1 envelope active dry yeast (2¼ tsp.)

2 Tbsp. olive oil

1 cup rye flour

2 cups flour, plus more

2 Tbsp. butter, melted

2 Tbsp. grated Parmesan

½ tsp. garlic powder

2 egg whites, beaten

4 Tbsp. caraway seeds

Filling

⅔ cup Thousand Island dressing

1 lb. turkey pastrami, thin sliced

16 slices swiss cheese

4 cups sauerkraut, drained

Baked Reuben Braid

My mom often makes something like this at family get-togethers. Even if you're not normally a fan of sauerkraut, I promise this deserves a try. —Emily

In a large bowl, add the sugar and salt to the hot water and then add the yeast. Allow the yeast to work for five minutes. Then stir in the olive oil and flours and work into a dough with your hands, adding more flour if needed to not stick. Knead into a smooth ball and then cover the bowl with a clean towel and place in a warm place.

Allow the dough to double in size, about 2 hours.

Preheat oven to 375°F. Punch dough down and split into two dough balls. On a floured cutting board, roll into a long oval (20 inches long, 15 inches wide), about ½-inch thick. Move dough oval to a baking sheet with parchment paper on it.

Using kitchen shears, make 8 two-inch deep cuts along each long side of the oval. Drizzle half of the dressing on the dough in the middle section between the cuts. Add half the pastrami and swiss, then top with half the sauerkraut. Start at the top of the oval and fold it down to where the cuts start. Now begin braiding the dough, starting with the left strip and folding it to the middle

Three-Cheese Frittata

Serves 4

- 1 tsp. butter
- 1 Tbsp. diced onion
- 6 eggs + 2 egg whites
- 2 Tbsp. milk
- ⅛ tsp. ground pepper
- ¼ tsp. salt
- 2 Tbsp. grated Asiago cheese
- 2 Tbsp. grated swiss cheese
- 2 Tbsp. grated provolone cheese
- dash parsley

Frittata. Omelette. Whatever you call it, it's delicious and wonderful any time of day. Feel free to experiment and add other types of cheeses or veggies, like spinach, tomatoes, green onions, asparagus, or zucchini. —Emily

Sauté onions in butter in a skillet over medium-high heat.

In a bowl, whisk eggs, egg whites, milk, pepper, and salt until frothy.

Add eggs to skillet and reduce heat to medium-low. Place a lid on the skillet and allow eggs to cook at least 5 minutes, until the eggs no longer look wet.

Remove lid and sprinkle cheeses and parsley on top, and allow cheese to just melt.

Remove from heat and cut into triangle slices, and serve while warm.

Provolone is an Italian cow's-milk cheese with a firm texture and tangy flavor. It is often smoked and is a great cheese for cooking.

Pastrami Provolone Panini

This is a sandwich I had at a small diner and unexpectedly couldn't stop thinking about, so I decided to try to re-create it. It's marvelous for breakfast, lunch, or dinner. —Emily

Serves 4

Mayo

2 Tbsp. mayonnaise

2 Tbsp. sour cream

½ tsp. mustard

Sandwich

4 eggs

2 Tbsp. butter, divided

1 large tomato, sliced

salt and pepper to taste

8 thick slices of French bread or Texas Toast bread

8 oz. sliced pastrami

6 oz. sliced provolone cheese

2 oz. fresh spinach

Make the mayo by mixing the mayonnaise, sour cream, and mustard together in a small bowl. Set aside.

Cook the eggs sunny-side up over medium heat in a frying pan by carefully breaking the eggs into the pan, adding a tablespoon of water to the pan, and then covering with a lid and letting cook about 5 minutes. Egg yolks should be gooey but not runny.

Remove eggs from the pan and set aside on a plate. Add a tablespoon of butter to the frying pan and add slices of tomato (in a single layer) and salt and pepper. Flip after 1 minute.

Assemble the sandwich by spreading butter on the two outer sides of each pair of bread slices. Spread the mayo on each of the inner sides of bread. Pile pastrami, provolone, spinach, and tomatoes on the bread and top with the top piece of bread.

Place sandwich in a panini grill or in the frying pan and cook each side. Once cheese is melted, remove from grill or pan, and pull the top layer of bread off. Add the egg and replace the bread.

It takes about 10 pounds of milk to make 1 pound of cheese.

Serves 8

Dough

1¼ cup hot water

1 tsp. sugar

2 tsp. salt

1 envelope active dry yeast (2¼ tsp.)

2 Tbsp. olive oil

1 cup rye flour

2 cups flour, plus more

2 Tbsp. butter, melted

2 Tbsp. grated Parmesan

½ tsp. garlic powder

2 egg whites, beaten

4 Tbsp. caraway seeds

Filling

⅔ cup Thousand Island dressing

1 lb. turkey pastrami, thin sliced

16 slices swiss cheese

4 cups sauerkraut, drained

Baked Reuben Braid

My mom often makes something like this at family get-togethers. Even if you're not normally a fan of sauerkraut, I promise this deserves a try. —Emily

In a large bowl, add the sugar and salt to the hot water and then add the yeast. Allow the yeast to work for five minutes. Then stir in the olive oil and flours and work into a dough with your hands, adding more flour if needed to not stick. Knead into a smooth ball and then cover the bowl with a clean towel and place in a warm place.

Allow the dough to double in size, about 2 hours.

Preheat oven to 375°F. Punch dough down and split into two dough balls. On a floured cutting board, roll into a long oval (20 inches long, 15 inches wide), about ½-inch thick. Move dough oval to a baking sheet with parchment paper on it.

Using kitchen shears, make 8 two-inch deep cuts along each long side of the oval. Drizzle half of the dressing on the dough in the middle section between the cuts. Add half the pastrami and swiss, then top with half the sauerkraut. Start at the top of the oval and fold it down to where the cuts start. Now begin braiding the dough, starting with the left strip and folding it to the middle of the dough, then crossing the top right strip over the left strip. Repeat, crossing the strips over each other until you have only 1 strip on each side left. Fold the bottom of the oval up, and then braid the last two strips and tuck under the folder bottom.

Use a pastry brush to spread egg wash on braid. Sprinkle with caraway seeds. Bake for 35 minutes, or until dough starts turning golden brown. Roll out the other dough ball and repeat the process, using the rest of the dressing, pastrami, swiss cheese, and sauerkraut, and then bake. Cut into 2-inch strips and serve warm.

Swiss cheese gets its characteristic flavor and holes during its aging process; carbon dioxide bubbles form within the cheese wheel. Originally, these holes were seen as imperfections and manufacturers would try to press the bubbles out.

Filling

2/3 cup Thousand Island dressing

1 lb. turkey pastrami, thin sliced

16 slices swiss cheese

4 cups sauerkraut, drained

Chicken Apple Havarti Melt

Makes 6

- 12 slices sourdough bread, divided
- ½ cup butter, softened
- ½ cup mayonnaise
- 1½ Tbsp. mustard
- 2 pkgs. sliced Havarti cheese (2 slices per sandwich)
- 4 tart apples, sliced thin
- 3 Roma tomatoes, sliced
- 1 (13-oz.) pkg. deli sliced chicken, divided

When my husband and I first got our panini press, I was so excited that I wanted to make sandwiches right away. This is one of the first I made. We loved it so much, I had to include it in the book. —Whitney

Prepare bread by buttering every slice of bread (grill side).

Mix together mayonnaise and mustard. Spread mixture on all slices of bread (inside).

Layer one slice of cheese, apples, tomatoes, chicken, and another slice of cheese. Top with reserved slices of bread.

Cook one at a time in a medium frying pan over medium-low heat, turning as necessary until cheese melts and both sides of sandwiches are browned.

NOTE: If you have a sandwich press, grill sandwiches for about 6 minutes on medium-high heat, turning once, or until cheese is melted and bread is toasted.

Havarti cheese was developed near Copenhagen, Denmark.

Goat Cheese and Cabbage Tacos

I made these after trying something similar at a local taco shop. The fresh ingredients on the corn tortillas can't be beat. —Whitney

Makes 12 Tacos

- 1½ Tbsp. butter
- ½ cup minced shallots
- 1½ Tbsp. flour
- ⅛ cup milk
- 1 cup shredded Monterey jack cheese
- 1 cup shredded cheddar cheese
- pinch chili powder
- salt and pepper to taste
- 12 corn tortillas
- 2 cups shredded cabbage
- ½ cup sliced radishes
- ½ cup chopped cilantro
- 3 oz. crumbled goat cheese

Sauté shallots in butter until translucent in a medium saucepan over medium heat.

Add flour and stir until thickened.

Add milk, and heat until simmering.

Add cheeses slowly until melted, stirring constantly. Add chili powder, salt, and pepper. Stir to combine.

Heat corn tortillas one at a time in a small saucepan until warm and flexible.

Stuff each tortilla with cheese mixture, cabbage, radishes, cilantro, and goat cheese. Serve warm.

Goat cheese has been around for centuries. The properties of goat's milk give goat cheese its tangy flavor.

Ultimate Grilled Cheese Variations

Each recipe makes 6

Three-Cheese

- 12 slices sourdough or rye bread, divided
- ½ cup butter, softened
- 1 pkg. sliced cheddar cheese
- 1 pkg. sliced swiss cheese
- 1 cup Romano cheese

Prepare bread by buttering every slice on both sides. Layer cheeses on bread. Top with reserved slices of bread. Cook one at a time in a medium frying pan over medium-low heat, turning as necessary until cheese melts and both sides of sandwiches are browned.

NOTE: If you have a sandwich press, grill sandwiches for about 6 minutes on medium-high heat, turning once, or until cheese is melted and bread is toasted.

Caprese

- 12 slices French bread, divided
- ½ cup butter, softened
- 8 oz. sliced mozzarella cheese
- 4 tomatoes, sliced
- 1 cup basil, sliced
- balsamic vinegar
- salt and pepper to taste

Prepare bread by buttering every slice on both sides. Drizzle vinegar over the bread. Layer cheese, tomato, basil, and more cheese. Sprinkle salt and pepper over bread. Top with reserved slices of bread. Cook one at a time in a medium frying pan over medium-low heat, turning as necessary until cheese melts and both sides of sandwiches are browned.

NOTE: If you have a sandwich press, grill sandwiches for about 6 minutes on medium-high heat, turning once, or until cheese is melted and bread is toasted.

Bacon-Cheddar

Prepare bread by buttering every slice on both sides. Layer cheese, onion, and bacon. Top with reserved slices of bread. Cook one at a time in a medium frying pan over medium-low heat, turning as necessary until cheese melts and both sides of sandwiches are browned.

NOTE: If you have a sandwich press, grill sandwiches for about 6 minutes on medium-high heat, turning once, or until cheese is melted and bread is toasted.

Bacon-Cheddar

- 12 slices sourdough bread, divided
- ½ cup butter, softened
- 2 pkgs. sliced cheddar cheese
- ½ cup sliced red onions
- 8 slices bacon, cooked and crumbled

Jalapeño

- 12 slices sourdough bread, divided
- ½ cup butter, softened
- 1 (8-oz.) pkg. cream cheese, softened
- dash cumin
- dash garlic salt
- 1 (4-oz.) can diced jalapeños (or ½ cup diced fresh jalapeños)
- 1 pkg. sliced cheddar cheese
- 1 cup shredded mozzarella cheese

Jalapeño

Prepare bread by buttering every slice on both sides. Mix cream cheese with cumin and garlic salt. Then spread a light layer of cream cheese mixture on every other bread slice. Sprinkle jalapeños over top, followed by mozzarella and cheddar cheese. Top with reserved slices of bread. Cook one at a time in a medium frying pan over medium-low heat, turning as necessary until cheese melts and both sides of sandwiches are browned.

NOTE: If you have a sandwich press, grill sandwiches for about 6 minutes on medium-high heat, turning once, or until cheese is melted and bread is toasted.

Grilled cheese sandwiches are said to have originated in the 1920s. Cooked bread and cheese dishes have been around for centuries.

Stromboli

My sweet mother-in-law introduced me to this recipe and patiently taught me how to braid the bread. This is always a crowd pleaser! —Emily

In a large bowl, add the sugar and salt to the hot water and then add the yeast. Allow the yeast to work for five minutes. Then stir in the olive oil and flour and work into a dough with your hands, adding more flour if needed to not stick. Knead into a smooth ball and then cover the bowl with a clean towel and place in a warm spot.

Allow the dough to double in size, about 2 hours.

Preheat oven to 375°F. Punch dough down and split into two dough balls. On a floured cutting board, roll into a long oval (20 inches long, 15 inches wide), about ½-inch thick. Move dough oval to a baking sheet with parchment paper on it.

Using kitchen shears, make 8 two-inch deep cuts along each long side of the oval. Now spoon half of the sauce on to the dough in the middle section between the cuts. Add half the meat and half the mozzarella on top of the sauce. Start at the top of the oval and fold it down to where the cuts start. Now begin braiding the dough, starting with the left strip and folding it to the middle of the dough, then crossing the top right strip over the left strip. Repeat, crossing the strips over each other until you have only 1 strip on each side left. Fold the bottom of the oval up, and then braid the last two strips and tuck under the folder bottom.

Use a pastry brush to spread melted butter over the top of the stromboli. Sprinkle with Parmesan cheese and garlic powder. Bake for 15 minutes, or until dough starts turning golden brown. Roll out the other dough ball and repeat the process, using the rest of the sauce, meat, and cheese, and then bake. Cut into 2-inch strips and serve warm.

Parmesan cheese is known as "the king of cheeses" and was first produced by Benedictine monks over a thousand years ago!

Serves 6

Dough

1¼ cup hot water

1 tsp. sugar

2 tsp. salt

1 envelope active dry yeast (2¼ tsp.)

2 Tbsp. olive oil

3 cups flour, plus more

2 Tbsp. butter, melted

2 Tbsp. grated Parmesan cheese

½ tsp. garlic powder

Filling

16 oz. marinara sauce or alfredo sauce

12 oz. Italian sausage or diced cooked chicken

8 oz. mozzarella cheese, shredded

Seafood Mac & Cheese

Serves 8 to 10

- 1 (16-oz.) pkg. uncooked pasta (you can even use multigrain pasta in this recipe)
- ½ cup butter
- ½ med. onion, chopped
- 1 tsp. minced garlic
- ½ cup flour
- 4 cups 2% milk
- 1 tsp. sea salt
- ¼ tsp. ground pepper
- ½ tsp. garlic powder
- ½ tsp. onion powder
- ¼ tsp. nutmeg
- ¼ tsp. paprika
- 1½ lb. coarsely chopped seafood (like imitation crab meat, canned clams, canned tiny shrimp)
- 3 cups shredded cheese, divided (a combination of sharp cheddar, Parmesan, and Gruyère works well)
- bread crumbs
- parsley

I love this recipe because it seems decadent and expensive, but it uses mostly canned seafood, so you're not breaking the bank. —Emily

Preheat oven to 400°F. In a pot of salted, boiling water, cook pasta to al dente, and then drain and set aside.

Melt butter in a medium saucepan. Add onion and garlic and sauté until tender. Add flour and stir constantly. Then whisk in milk. Bring to a boil and then turn down heat to a simmer.

Add salt, pepper, garlic and onion powder, nutmeg, and paprika. Cook until sauce thickens and then turn off heat.

Fold the sauce mixture, seafood, and 2 cups of the cheese into the pasta. Then transfer into a shallow baking dish. Top with remaining cheese and then sprinkle with bread crumbs and parsley.

Bake 15 minutes, or until cheese on top is bubbling.

Gruyère cheese is a hard, yellow cheese from Switzerland. It is a slightly sweet, nutty cheese that works well in baked dishes.

Havarti Jalapeño Mac & Cheese

Even if you don't love spicy food, the creaminess of this casserole really balances the heat out. And if you want more heat, add more jalapeños and don't remove all the seeds. —Emily

Serves 6 to 8

- 3 cups uncooked macaroni noodles
- 4 oz. cream cheese
- 1 cup milk
- 1 cup cream
- ½ tsp. onion salt
- ¼ tsp. pepper
- 2 jalapeños, sliced and seeded
- 8 oz. pepper jack cheese, shredded
- 8 oz. Havarti cheese, shredded
- bread crumbs
- grated Parmesan cheese

Preheat oven to 400°F. In a pot of salted, boiling water, cook pasta to al dente and then drain and set aside.

Melt cream cheese in a medium saucepan. Whisk in milk and cream. Bring to a boil and then turn down heat to a simmer. Add onion salt and pepper.

Cook until sauce thickens and then turn off heat. Fold the sauce mixture, jalapeños, and the pepper jack and Havarti cheeses into the pasta. Then transfer into a shallow baking dish.

Top with Parmesan cheese and then sprinkle with bread crumbs.

Bake 15 minutes, or until the top gets golden brown and bubbly.

Havarti cheese is a white, semisoft Danish cheese with a buttery flavor and is made from cow's milk. It's super creamy and one of our favorite cheeses in the world.

Slow Cooker Mac & Cheese

A family favorite! This classic recipe is better than any of the boxed stuff. —Whitney

Serves 6 to 8

- 1 (16-oz.) pkg. elbow macaroni
- ½ cup butter
- 1 (10.75-oz.) can condensed cheddar cheese soup
- 2½ cups shredded sharp cheddar cheese
- ½ cup shredded mozzarella cheese
- ½ cup plain Greek yogurt or sour cream
- ½ tsp salt
- 1 cup milk
- ½ tsp dry mustard
- ½ tsp black pepper

Spray slow cooker with cooking spray. Add salt to a large pot of water and bring to a boil. Cook macaroni 6-8 minutes until cooked through but still firm (al dente). Drain pasta and set aside.

Melt butter over medium heat in a large saucepan. Add soup and stir until well mixed. Add cheese and stir until melted. Combine cheese mixture, yogurt or sour cream, salt, milk, mustard, and pepper in slow cooker.

Add drained macaroni and stir to combine.

Cook for 2–2½ hours on low, stirring occasionally. Add milk if needed to thin out sauce. Serve hot.

"White cheddar" does not include annatto, the extract used to give cheddar its customary color.

Homestyle Mac & Cheese

Serves 6

- ¾ (16-oz.) pkg. uncooked macaroni
- 3 Tbsp. butter
- ¼ cup flour
- 2½ cups milk
- 1 tsp. mustard
- ¼ tsp. pepper
- ½ tsp. garlic powder
- ½ tsp. onion powder
- ½ tsp. salt
- 1 cup shredded Muenster cheese
- 1 cup shredded sharp or white cheddar cheese
- ½ cup grated Parmesan cheese
- 1 Tbsp. bread crumbs

If you're looking for the ultimate comfort food, this is it. —Emily

Preheat oven to 350°F. Cook pasta to al dente in a pot of salted boiling water. Drain and set aside.

In a medium saucepan, melt butter and add flour to make a roux. Add milk, a bit at a time, stirring constantly. Add mustard, pepper, garlic powder, onion powder, and salt. Allow sauce to thicken, stirring constantly.

Combine the sauce, pasta, and two-thirds of the grated cheeses in a casserole dish. Top with remaining grated cheeses and bread crumbs.

Bake for 15 minutes, or until cheese is bubbling and browning.

Muenster cheese is made from cow's milk and has an off-white inside and orange rind that is perfect for melting.

Baked Five-Cheese Ziti

Maybe it's obvious by now, but I love Italian food. It's my ultimate comfort food. Give me a little mozzarella and pasta and I'm happy.
—Emily

Serves 6 to 8

- 1 (16-oz.) pkg. uncooked ziti or penne pasta
- 4 cups tomato sauce
- 1 tsp. basil
- ½ tsp. oregano
- ½ tsp. thyme
- ¼ tsp. pepper
- ½ tsp. onion powder
- ½ tsp. garlic powder
- 1 cup ricotta cheese
- 2 cups grated mozzarella cheese
- ½ cup grated Fontina cheese
- ½ cup grated Romano cheese
- ½ cup shredded Parmesan cheese
- dash of parsley

Preheat oven to 350°F. In a pot of salted boiling water, cook pasta just to al dente so noodles are still slightly chewy. Drain and set aside.

In a large bowl, mix together tomato sauce and all seasonings. Fold in ricotta, pasta, and all cheeses except the Parmesan.

Pour into a deep casserole dish and top with the Parmesan and parsley. Bake for 25 minutes. Turn on the broiler for the last 2 minutes so cheese gets bubbly.

Fontina cheese has been made in Italy since the twelfth century and is made from cow's milk.

Cheesy Spinach Fettuccine Alfredo

Makes 6

- 1 (16-oz.) pkg. fettuccine
- 1 (8-oz.) pkg. cream cheese
- 1 (8-oz.) pkg. spinach, rinsed and dried (about two large handfuls)
- ½ cup milk
- ½ cup Romano cheese
- ½ cup grated Parmesan cheese
- Italian seasoning to taste
- salt and pepper to taste

Okay, so this isn't really "authentic" Italian food, but I sure love it and it is quite a bit healthier than the restaurant variety. The cheeses all work together to create a tangy, smooth sauce that pairs perfectly with the spinach. You can also add grilled chicken for an extra flavor boost. —Whitney

Cook fettuccine according to instructions on package, and then drain and set aside.

Melt cream cheese in large saucepan over medium heat, stirring frequently. Add spinach and cook until wilted. Add milk and cook until smooth, stirring frequently.

Add remaining cheeses and spices and cook until all cheeses are melted and sauce is smooth. Combine with fettuccine and serve.

Sprinkle with more Parmesan cheese before serving if desired.

Parmesan cheese is often used as a seasoning for Italian dishes. Parmigiano-Reggiano is the official name of Parmesan cheese.

Broccoli Cheddar Soup

Serves 6

- ½ cup butter
- ½ medium onion, diced
- ½ cup flour
- 1 cup cream
- 2 cups milk
- 2 cans vegetable broth
- 1 tsp. mustard
- ¼ tsp. pepper
- ½ tsp. salt
- ½ tsp. onion powder
- 1 lb. fresh broccoli florets, chopped finely
- 1½ cup shredded sharp or white cheddar cheese
- ½ cup grated Parmesan cheese

This is especially delicious served in a bread bowl on a wintry day. —Emily

In a large pot, sauté the onion in the butter until soft. Add the flour to create a roux.

Slowly add the cream and milk and stir constantly, bringing to a simmer. Add the vegetable broth, mustard, pepper, salt, and onion powder.

While still stirring frequently, allow the soup to boil and thicken (up to 20 minutes). Once it has reached desired thickness, add broccoli and cheeses.

Simmer for 10 minutes until broccoli is soft but still bright green.

Cheddar cheese is the second most popular cheese in the United States (behind mozzarella). It is the most popular cheese in the United Kingdom, which is where this cheese was originally developed back in the twelfth century!

White Lasagna

This is based on my Grandma Chambers's recipe and is such a fun and delicious variation on traditional lasagna. —Emily

Preheat oven to 350°F. In a pot of salted boiling water, cook lasagna noodles to al dente. Drain and set aside.

In a saucepan over medium heat, melt butter. Add flour and stir constantly to make a roux. Add the lemon juice, garlic salt, and chicken bouillon. Add the milk, a bit at a time, and stir constantly until sauce thickens. Stir in chicken and remove from heat. This makes the béchamel sauce.

In a bowl, combine ricotta and cottage cheese, ¼ cup of the Parmesan cheese, and parsley. Layer a third of the lasagna noodles in the bottom of a 9x13 baking dish. Spread a third the ricotta mixture over the noodles and sprinkle on a third of the mozzarella. Then spoon a third of the chicken béchamel sauce on top.

Repeat layers two more times. Top with the remaining ½ cup Parmesan cheese.

Cottage cheese curds are washed before packaging to rinse away the natural acidic flavor, making cottage cheese mild and slightly sweet tasting.

Serves 6

- 9 lasagna noodles
- 2 Tbsp. butter
- ¼ cup flour
- 2 tsp. lemon juice
- 1 tsp. garlic salt
- 1 chicken bouillon cube
- 3 cups milk
- 2 cups cooked and cubed chicken
- 8 oz. ricotta cheese
- 8 oz. cottage cheese
- ¾ cup shredded Parmesan cheese, divided
- 1 tsp. parsley
- 2 cups shredded mozzarella cheese

Serves 6

Meat Sauce

1 Tbsp. olive oil

½ large onion, chopped finely

2 tsp. minced garlic

1 lb. ground lamb (or lean ground beef or pork)

1¼ cup tomato sauce

⅛ tsp. cinnamon

⅛ tsp. cloves

½ tsp. rosemary

½ tsp. thyme

½ tsp. oregano

½ tsp. marjoram

Béchamel Sauce

4 Tbsp. butter

4 Tbsp. flour

3 cups milk

¼ tsp. nutmeg

¼ tsp. pepper

1 tsp. salt

2 egg yolks

¼ cup grated Parmesan cheese

Pasta Layer

10 oz. penne pasta, cooked to al dente and drained

4 oz. feta cheese, cubed and then smashed with a fork

Topping

½ cup grated Parmesan cheese

1 tsp. parsley

Pastitsio (Greek Lasagna)

One of my fondest childhood memories is going to an amazing and authentic restaurant in Detroit's Greektown with my family. This recipe was inspired by those memories. —Emily

Preheat oven to 350°F. In a large skillet, prepare the meat sauce by sautéing the onion and garlic in the olive oil until tender. Add ground meat and tomato sauce, breaking up the meat finely with a spatula. Mix in the cinnamon, cloves, rosemary, thyme, oregano, and marjoram and let simmer 5 minutes.

In a separate skillet, make the béchamel sauce by melting the butter over medium heat. Add the flour and work in to create a paste. Add the milk a bit at a time, stirring continuously to work out any lumps. Add the nutmeg, pepper, and salt. Simmer while stirring until the sauce thickens. Remove skillet from heat and quickly whisk in egg yolks and then Parmesan cheese.

In a deep baking dish, layer half of the cooked pasta and smashed feta cheese. Spoon half of the meat sauce on top of that and even out. Then top with half of the béchamel sauce. Repeat layering pasta, meat sauce, and béchamel sauce, using the second half of everything. Top with the grated Parmesan cheese and parsley.

Bake for 45 minutes, until cheese on top is golden brown and bubbling.

According to European Union regulations, only feta cheese manufactured in Macedonia, Thrace, Thessaly, Central Mainland Greece, the Peloponnese, and Lesvos can be called "feta."

Cheese Enchiladas

You might be skeptical about enchiladas without meat, but the mixture of cheeses with the enchilada sauce creates a vegetarian-friendly delight. —Whitney

Makes 12

- 1½ Tbsp. butter
- 1½ Tbsp. flour
- ⅛ cup milk
- 3 cups shredded Monterey Jack cheese, divided
- 3 cup shredded cheddar cheese, divided
- 1 cup sour cream
- pinch chili powder
- pinch cumin
- salt and pepper to taste
- 12 flour tortillas
- 1 (10-oz.) can green enchilada sauce

Heat oven to 350°F. Melt butter in a medium saucepan over medium heat. Add flour and stir until thickened. Add milk and heat until simmering, stirring occasionally.

Add 2 cups each of Monterey Jack and cheddar cheeses slowly until melted, stirring constantly. Add chili powder, salt, and pepper. Pour half of the enchilada sauce into a 9x13 baking dish. Stuff each tortilla with melted cheese mixture and sour cream. Line enchiladas in dish. Top with the rest of the enchilada sauce and remaining cup of cheese.

Cover with foil and bake for 20 minutes. Remove foil and bake for 20 more minutes until edges of enchiladas are browned and cheeses are all melted. Serve hot.

Pepper jack cheese is also great in this recipe. Interestingly, pepper jack cheese is just Monterey Jack cheese with different peppers added in during the production process.

Pizza Variations

Each recipe makes 2 pizzas

Easy Pizza Dough

Serves 4–6

Dough

- 3 tsp. active dry yeast
- 1 cup warm water
- 1 tsp. sugar
- 2 Tbsp. olive oil
- 1 tsp. salt
- 1 Tbsp. pizza or Italian seasoning
- 3 cups flour

Dissolve yeast and sugar in water and let sit until bubbly. Add oil, salt, and pizza seasoning, and stir to combine. Add flour 1 cup at a time and mix until all incorporated. If needed, add more flour until dough isn't sticky. Place dough in an oiled bowl, cover, and let rise for 15–20 minutes. Turn dough and let rise for 15 more minutes. Use with your favorite pizza recipe.

Easy Margherita

Pizza

- 1 recipe Easy Pizza Dough (or your favorite recipe)
- 1 small can pizza sauce
- 8 oz. fresh buffalo mozzarella cheese (balls)
- 2 Roma tomatoes, sliced (or chopped, I haven't decided)
- ⅓ cup sliced fresh basil
- drizzle of balsamic vinegar
- salt and pepper to taste

I love all types of pizza, and this one is especially great. The balsamic vinegar adds a fantastic tang to make this pizza anything but ordinary.—Whitney

Divide pizza dough into two balls, and line 2 baking sheets with parchment paper. Stretch pizza dough and place on baking sheets. Spread a thin layer of pizza sauce over both pizzas and then layer toppings (all except vinegar) to your taste, ending with basil. Bake at 450°F for 15 minutes, or until crust is golden and cheese is melted. Before serving, drizzle vinegar over the top and add salt and pepper if desired.

If you don't have buffalo mozzarella, you can substitute shredded mozzarella just fine.

Caramelized Onion and Goat Cheese

Serves 4–6

- 1 recipe Easy Pizza Dough (or your favorite recipe)
- 2 Tbsp. butter
- 1 medium Vidalia onion, sliced
- 1 jar basil pesto (found near the spaghetti sauce in the supermarket)
- 2 cups shredded mozzarella cheese, divided
- 3 oz. goat cheese, crumbled
- salt and pepper to taste

The flavor of this pizza is interesting . . . in a great way. The tanginess of the goat cheese pairs perfectly with sweetness of the Vidalia onions. —Whitney

Divide pizza dough into two balls, and line 2 baking sheets with parchment paper. Stretch pizza dough and place on baking sheets.

Heat butter in a medium saucepan over medium heat, add onions, and cook until browned (not burned!). The natural sugars in the onions will caramelize them. Remove from heat and set aside.

Spread a thin layer of pesto over both pizzas and then layer toppings to your taste, ending with crumbled goat cheese.

Bake at 450°F for 15 minutes, or until crust is golden and cheese is melted. Before serving, add salt and pepper if desired.

Barbecue Chicken

The cilantro totally makes this pizza. It complements all the flavors and adds an interesting twist. —Whitney

Serves 4–6

- 1 recipe Easy Pizza Dough
- 2 chicken breasts, cooked and shredded
- ½ cup barbecue sauce, divided
- ½ cup cilantro, chopped and divided
- 1 red onion, sliced
- 1 cup shredded mozzarella cheese, divided
- 1 cup shredded cheddar cheese, divided

Divide pizza dough into two balls, and line 2 baking sheets with parchment paper. Stretch pizza dough and place on baking sheets. Spread a thin layer of barbecue sauce over both pizzas and then layer toppings to your taste, reserving cilantro.

Bake at 450°F for 11 minutes. Add cilantro and then bake for about 5 minutes, or until crust is golden and cheese is melted.

Before serving, add more cilantro if desired.

Modern pizza was developed in Naples, Italy. The exact etymology of "pizza" is unknown, though several languages suggest possibilities.

Bacon-Wrapped Cheese-Stuffed Chicken Breasts

With only five ingredients, this recipe is simple, but the flavor is anything but. I like to make this when I don't feel like cooking for hours but still want something special. —Whitney

Serves 8

- 8 chicken breast halves
- 1 pkg. Italian seasoning
- ½ cup goat cheese
- ½ cup blue cheese
- 1 pkg. bacon

Marinate chicken in Italian seasoning for at least an hour, but overnight is preferable.

Preheat oven to 350°F. Pound chicken breast halves thin, to about ¾ inch.

Place cheeses in center of chicken breasts and roll up and secure with toothpicks.

Wrap chicken breasts in two slices of bacon in a crisscross pattern and secure with toothpicks.

Bake for 50–55 minutes, or until juices run clear and bacon is browned. The thicker the bacon, the longer the chicken needs to bake. Drain off fat, remove toothpicks, and serve warm.

Goat cheese has been around for centuries and could be one of the oldest dairy products.

Chicken Cheese Quesadillas

Serves 8

- 2 chicken breasts
- 1 pkg. taco seasoning
- 1 cup pepper jack cheese
- 1 cup Mexican blend cheese
- 8 uncooked tortillas
- salsa, optional
- sour cream, optional
- avocados, optional

These are a go-to dish in my house. The uncooked tortillas really make these quesadillas shine. —Whitney

Place chicken breasts and taco seasoning in a slow cooker and cook on low for 8 hours or on high for 3–4 hours. Shred chicken. Cook tortillas according to package instructions. Fill half of each tortilla with cheeses, chicken, and other fillings.

Cook in a frying pan on medium heat until cheese is melted, about 8 minutes, turning once, or cook in a panini press on medium for about 6 minutes, until cheese is melted.

Serve with chips, guacamole, salsa, and sour cream if desired.

NOTE: If you don't have uncooked tortillas, regular ones are fine to use, but make sure you heat them up first.

Pepper jack cheese is a variant of Monterey Jack cheese.

Blue Ribbon Cheeseburgers

Cheeseburgers with blue cheese are my favorite, rivaled perhaps only by my love of cheeseburgers with goat cheese. This recipe adds a gourmet twist to a simple meal. —Whitney

Serves 8

- 2 Tbsp. Worcestershire sauce
- 2 pounds ground beef or turkey
- McCormick Grill Mates seasoning or seasoned salt, optional
- 1 cup blue cheese
- 1 pkg. mushrooms
- 2 Tbsp. butter
- ½ tsp. salt
- shredded spring mix
- sliced tomato
- pickles
- 8 brioche hamburger buns

Combine meat with Worcestershire sauce. Divide into 8 ¼-pound patties. Set aside.

Sauté mushrooms in butter in small batches so they can brown. Add salt and cook until browned.

Sprinkle each side of burgers with Grill Mates seasoning or seasoned salt. Cook hamburger patties as desired.

Prepare buns. Add spring mix, tomato, and pickles. Add cooked patties to buns. Top with grilled mushrooms and blue cheese. Serve with fries or chips.

Another option is to mix the blue cheese in with the ground beef. The cheese will cook out a little, but the flavor will permeate the burger. If you must, you can swap out the mushrooms with bacon . . . but mushrooms are the best. You can also substitute chicken breasts, pounded thin, for the hamburger patties.

Blue cheese gets its distinct color from bacteria being added to the cheese during production.

Pepper Cheesesteak Sandwiches

The peppers in this dish really bring out the flavor of the meat and make the sandwiches especially tasty. If you don't like peppers, you can omit them for a more traditional sandwich. Don't skip the provolone, though! —Whitney

Serves 6

- ¼ cup Italian seasoning
- 1 lb. thin-cut beef, sliced into strips
- 3 Tbsp. butter
- 1 green peppers, diced
- 1 red pepper, diced
- ½ medium yellow onion, diced
- ½ (8-oz.) pkg. mushrooms, optional
- salt and pepper to taste
- ½ cup butter, softened
- 2 tsp. garlic powder
- 6 hoagie rolls, split
- 1 pkg. sliced provolone cheese (10–12 slices)
- 1 pkg. sliced cheddar cheese

Heat oven to broil. Rub Italian seasoning into meat. Set aside. Sauté vegetables in butter in a large saucepan over medium-high heat. Cook until soft.

Add beef and cook until browned. Mix butter and garlic powder and spread on hoagie rolls. Place open rolls under broiler and toast lightly (about 1 minute 30 seconds). Remove from oven.

Spread meat on rolls, cover with two slices of cheese, and return to oven. Toast until cheese is melted, about 2 minutes. Serve with chips.

NOTE: Make sure you watch the toasting bread carefully to prevent burning.

Provolone cheese or the product Cheez Whiz are offered as options on traditional Philadelphia cheesesteaks.

Cheddar Cheese Soup

This soup is one of my favorites. I especially like it with crusty bread and a side salad. —Whitney

Serves 6

2 Tbsp. butter
½ yellow onion, diced
2 Tbsp. flour
2 cups chicken broth
1 cup milk
2 cups shredded cheddar cheese
bacon bits for garnish

Melt butter in a large saucepan over medium heat. Add onions and sauté until translucent. Add flour and stir until thickened. Slowly add chicken broth and stir to incorporate fully until adding in more. Add milk and stir to combine.

Bring soup to a boil over medium-high heat. Remove from heat. Add cheese slowly, about a handful at a time, and make sure cheese melts before adding more.

Serve with bacon bits on top, if desired.

There are more than 2,000 varieties of cheese. Over 20 million metric tons of cheese is produced every year worldwide.

"CHEESE HAS ALWAYS BEEN A FOOD THAT BOTH SOPHISTICATED AND SIMPLE HUMANS LOVE."
– M. F. K. Fisher

Desserts

Cream Cheese Stuffed French Toast

This decadent dish is a mouthwatering breakfast or dessert. If I ever run a bed and breakfast, this will be on the menu! —Emily

Serves 4 to 6

- 1 loaf French bread (16 slices)
- 6 eggs
- 1 cup milk
- 3 tsp. vanilla extract, divided
- 2 tsp. cinnamon, divided
- 1 (8-oz.) package cream cheese, softened
- 2 Tbsp. powdered sugar

Leave the French bread slices out for several hours or over night so they dry out a bit beforehand. Set aside.

Whisk together the eggs, milk, 2 teaspoons of the vanilla, and 1 teaspoon of the cinnamon in a shallow, wide dish.

In a separate bowl, mix together the cream cheese, powdered sugar, remaining teaspoon of vanilla, and remaining teaspoon of cinnamon. Warm up a frying pan on medium heat.

Spread the cream cheese mixture fairly thin (about ⅛-inch thick) between 2 slices of bread. Dip both outer faces of the stuffed French toast in the egg mixture and then place in the frying pan. Flip after about 2 minutes, or until the facedown side has started to brown.

Repeat with all the French bread. Serve while still warm with maple syrup, whipped cream, and fruit.

Cream cheese is actually just one type of the "cream cheeses." Other types of "cream cheeses" are ricotta, mascarpone, and cottage cheese.

MYSHA DENSON

Honey Chèvre Panna Cotta

Panna cotta is a dessert that originated in Northern Italy, traditionally using eggs, cream, and honey. It is a divinely creamy and silky dessert that will wow guests with not too much work. —Emily

Serves 6

1 packet unflavored gelatin powder (such as Knox)

½ cup milk

2 cups cream

2 Tbsp. honey plus more to drizzle

2 Tbsp. sugar

4 oz. chèvre, softened

1 tsp. vanilla extract

½ cup buttermilk

blackberries to garnish

In a small bowl, dissolve gelatin in milk.

In a medium saucepan over medium heat, combine the cream, honey, and sugar. Bring to just a simmer and then turn off the heat.

Whisk in the chèvre until totally smooth. Then whisk in the gelatin-milk mixture, vanilla, and buttermilk. Strain the hot mixture through a mesh strainer to get rid of any chèvre lumps.

Pour into 6 greased ramekins or small dishes and chill for at least 4 hours.

Unmold panna cotta onto plates and garnish with drizzled honey and blackberries.

Chèvre *is the French name for goat cheese.*

Hazelnut Cocoa Tiramisu

I had a roommate in college who had lived in France and I wanted to make tiramisu for her birthday. The problem was, I didn't feel comfortable serving raw eggs, which most tiramisu recipes use, and I wasn't old enough to buy rum. Not to mention that I was such a chocaholic that I thought it was a crying shame to use coffee instead of something like hot cocoa. That's when I first started developing this coffee, rum, and raw egg–free tiramisu recipe. . . . Tiramisu purists: try this before you judge. —Emily

Serves 6

- 1½ cups water
- 2 Tbsp. instant coffee substitute powder (such as Postum, Caro, or Pero)
- 5 Tbsp. hazelnut hot cocoa powder, divided
- 1 (7 oz.) package lady finger cookies
- 16 oz. mascarpone
- 1 pint cream, divided
- ½ cup sugar
- 4 egg yolks
- ½ tsp. rum flavoring
- 2 Tbsp. powdered sugar
- chocolate curls

In a tall mug, boil the water in the microwave. Add the coffee or coffee substitute powder and 4 tablespoons of the hot cocoa powder and stir. Fully submerge each lady finger into this cocoa liquid for no more than 5 seconds and then lay in the bottom of an 8x8 casserole dish. Break the cookies in length to cover the whole bottom of the dish (you should use half the package of lady fingers and reserve the other half for another layer). Set the casserole dish aside.

In a medium saucepan, soften the mascarpone cheese over medium heat. Add ½ cup of the cream, the sugar, the egg yolks, and the rum flavoring. Stir constantly using a whisk, making sure to scrape the bottom of the pan. Bring to a simmer, but not to a boil. Mixture should thicken and be a pale yellow color. Pour half of the custard over the prepared lady fingers in the casserole dish.

Now repeat, dipping the other half of the lady fingers and lay over the custard layer in the dish. Pour remaining custard over this second layer of lady fingers. Whip the remaining 1½ cup of the cream in a stand mixer or with a hand mixer until it starts to thicken. Add the powdered sugar and continue whipping until stiff peaks form. Spread the whipped cream over the top custard layer. Chill for at least 3 hours. Right before serving, sift the remaining hot cocoa powder over the top and garnish with chocolate curls.

Mascarpone (pronounced mah-skar-POH-nay) is an Italian cheese that is made from cream. It's somewhere between ricotta and cream cheese in texture and flavor.

MYSHA DENSON

Berry Mascarpone Trifle

This is such an elegant yet simple dessert. I often serve this at showers or outdoor parties during the summer while it's berry season. —Emily

Serves 8

3 cups cream

¾ cup powdered sugar

16 oz. mascarpone, softened

1½ lbs. strawberries, raspberries, blackberries, or a combination

¼ cup lemon juice

¼ cup sugar

1 (14-oz.) angel food cake, cubed

Whip the cream in a stand mixer until it starts to thicken. Add powdered sugar and then whip some more until soft peaks form. Fold in the softened mascarpone. Set aside.

Wash the berries and hull and slice if using strawberries. Toss the berries in the lemon juice and sugar.

In a large clear bowl, layer a third of the angel food cake cubes, a third of the mascarpone cream, and a third of the berries. Repeat the layers two more times, ending with the berries. Chill and serve.

Mascarpone ranges in texture from a clotted cream to softened butter and is an off-white color.

Dulce de Leche Cheesecake

Serves 6 to 8

Crust

9 graham cracker rectangles

¼ cup sugar

6 Tbsp. butter, melted

Cheesecake

1 envelope unflavored gelatin

½ cup boiling water

2 (8-oz.) pkgs. cream cheese, softened

½ cup sweetened condensed milk

4 tsp. lemon juice

1 tsp. caramel extract

Topping

½ cup sweetened condensed milk

chopped pecans

whipped cream

When it comes to cheesecake, I prefer a creamy texture as opposed to a baked, firmer texture. This recipe uses gelatin to set the cheesecake and is a variation of my mother-in-law's cheesecake. —Emily

Preheat oven to 375°F. Crush the graham crackers and then blend in the sugar. Toss with melted butter and press into an 8-inch pie plate. Bake for 7 minutes. Allow crust to cool.

In a bowl, dissolve the gelatin into the boiling water and let sit for 5 minutes. In a stand mixer, whip cream cheese several minutes until fluffy. Gradually add the sweetened condensed milk, lemon juice, and caramel extract, and then add the gelatin mixture and continue blending.

Pour into prepared pie crust. Chill 3 hours before serving. Top with drizzled sweetened condensed milk, chopped pecans, and whipped cream.

Cream cheese appears to have first developed in England in the 1500s, but it became especially popular in the 1870s in Philadelphia, Pennsylvania.

White Chocolate Cheesecake

This recipe is a tribute to my dad, who absolutely loves white chocolate. —Emily

Serves 6-8

Crust

9 graham cracker rectangles

¼ cup sugar

6 Tbsp. butter, melted

Cheesecake

1 envelope unflavored gelatin

½ cup boiling water

2 (8-oz.) pkgs. cream cheese, softened

¼ cup sugar

1 tsp. vanilla

1 Tbsp. lemon juice

1 (16-oz.) bag white chocolate chips (don't use Ghirardelli)

Preheat oven to 375°F. Crush the graham crackers and then blend in the sugar. Toss with melted butter and press into a 9-inch pie plate. Bake for 7 minutes. Allow crust to cool.

In a bowl, dissolve the gelatin into the boiling water and let sit for 5 minutes. In a stand mixer, whip cream cheese several minutes until fluffy. Add the sugar, vanilla, and lemon juice and mix.

In a double boiler, melt the white chocolate until there are no more lumps. Add immediately to the cream cheese mixture and blend well on a high speed. Then add the gelatin mixture and continue blending. Pour into prepared pie crust.

Chill at least 3 hours before serving to allow the cheesecake to properly set. Top with fresh raspberries.

Cream cheese was first introduced in the United States in 1872 by a New York dairyman. It's a soft, unripened cheese made from cow's milk.

Serves 8

- 2 (8-oz.) pkgs. cream cheese, softened
- 2 cups milk
- 3 cups cream
- 1 tsp. caramel extract
- 2 tsp. vanilla extract
- 1½ cup sugar
- ½ cup caramel topping
- 1 tsp. coarse salt

Salted Caramel Ice Cream

Even though I feel like the "salted caramel" flavor trend was developed purely by an ice cream accident, I do think it's inspired. And, hey, if a bit of the salt gets in the ice cream, no one will even know. —Emily

In a stand mixer, whip the cream cheese several minutes.

Add the milk and blend together until there are no lumps. Put the cream cheese mixture in an ice cream canister, and add the cream, extracts, and sugar. Follow ice cream maker instructions.

Garnish dished ice cream with caramel topping and coarse salt.

Cream cheese is named for its creamy, spreadable texture. It's mildly tangy and slightly salty.

Raspberry Ricotta Swirl Brownies

These are the gooiest brownies you'll ever eat. The ricotta makes them superbly moist. —Emily

Serves 20

Brownies
½ cup butter, softened
1 cup sugar
2 eggs
2 Tbsp. oil
1 tsp. vanilla
½ cup flour
½ cup cocoa powder
½ tsp. baking powder
¼ tsp. salt

Ricotta Swirl
8 oz. ricotta cheese
⅓ cup sweetened condensed milk
⅓ cup sugar
1 egg
3 Tbsp. flour
½ tsp. baking powder
½ tsp. vanilla

Raspberry Swirl
6 Tbsp. seedless raspberry jam

Preheat oven to 350°F. In a stand mixer, cream butter and sugar together until fluffy. Add eggs, oil, and vanilla; mix. In a separate bowl, combine flour, cocoa, baking powder, and salt. Add to mixer and blend until dry ingredients are incorporated.

In another bowl, mix together all Ricotta Swirl ingredients.

Pour half of the brownie mixture into a 9 x 13 baking dish and spread to cover the bottom. Pour the Ricotta Swirl mixture over top and carefully spread to edges. Next, drop the remaining brownie mixture in blobs over top to form islands. Finally, drizzle raspberry jam sporadically around. Using a knife, carefully swirl the blade around (but not so much that everything blends together).

Bake for 45 minutes, or until toothpick inserted in the middle comes out clean.

Ricotta (which literally means "re-cooked") is an Italian sheep's-milk cheese made by coagulating proteins from the leftover whey.

Sandwich Cookie Dessert Ball

Makes 2 Cookie Balls

- 1 pkg. chocolate sandwich cookies
- 2 (8-oz.) pkgs. cream cheese, softened
- 1 (8-oz.) pkg. mini chocolate chips

The cookies mixed with the cream cheese creates magic in your mouth. Better double the recipe! —Whitney

Place cookies in blender or food processor and pulse until cookies are completely pulverized.

Blend the cream cheese and cookies in a medium mixing bowl. Mix until well combined—and this might mean using your hands instead of a spoon.

Divide and shape into two balls. Roll each ball in mini chocolate chips.

Serve with graham crackers, vanilla wafers, or other items of your choice.

Cheese is an excellent source of protein, calcium, and phosphorus. It also has an antibacterial effect that helps protect tooth enamel. It's the saturated fat in some cheeses that sometimes give it a bad reputation.

Fruit Fluff

My whole family loves this dessert dip. I serve it with a variety of fruits for a delicious summertime treat! —Whitney

Serves 24

1 (8-oz.) pkg. mixed berry whipped cream cheese (any whipped fruity flavor will do)

1 (8-oz.) jar marshmallow fluff

1 (8-oz.) pkg. frozen dairy dessert (Cool Whip), thawed in fridge

Place cream cheese in medium mixing bowl, add marshmallow fluff and frozen dairy dessert and whip until fluffy. Chill until ready to serve. Serve with your favorite fruit.

NOTE: You can whip by hand or use the whisk or cookie paddle attachments on a stand mixer.

A New York dairyman was the first to mass-produce cream cheese.

About the Authors

Emily Woodbury Chambers first fell in love with cheese when she lived in Germany for a semester in college (though growing up in a family of good cooks and food snobs was probably a contributing factor). It was after a scrumtrulescent bite of specialty Swedish cheese that she knew life would never be the same. While not a trained chef, Emily enjoys throwing parties, barbecues, and all other types of get-togethers where people gather around food. She cites her most influential food inspirations as her mom, aunt Michele, and Food Network. She and her husband, Joe, currently live in Utah.

Whitney Lindsley hails from northwest Arkansas, where she developed a deep love of food (and cheese), having learned from foodie parents the intricacies of all things delicious. Never a picky eater, Whitney tries new foods every chance she gets, and if the chosen dish has cheese in the title—even better! As a food preparation teaching assistant in college, she was able to pass on her love of food to others. She and her husband, Richard, currently live in Utah, where together they frequently enjoy international cuisine, bacon cheeseburgers, and grilled cheese sandwiches.

Whitney and Emily blog at thegoudagirls.com.

0 26575 15907 3